MW01623836

TO

FROM

DATE

"Lord, I need You"...isn't that the essence of so many of our prayers? And it is a good prayer because Jesus is everything that we need! We cannot ask for or imagine more.

When I bow my head and surrender it all, I have realized that "I can't and only He can." And in that moment, my heart is open for what He wants to do in my life.

I invite you to join me in praying these prayers with an open and expectant heart. Let us see how He will answer us. And as we read the Scriptures, let us look for His heart as He changes ours.

Sandy Lynam Clough

Prayers From a Humble Heart

Devotional Journal

SANDY LYNAM CLOUGH

Lord, I don't want to come before You with reckless, demanding words. Teach me to pray. Fill my heart with words You want me to pray and the kind of pleas You want to answer. AMEN

Let the words of my mouth and the meditation of my heart
Be acceptable *and* pleasing in Your sight, O LORD,
my [firm, immovable] rock and my Redeemer.
Psalm 19:14 AMP

Then you will call upon Me and come and pray to Me, and I will listen to you.
Jeremiah 29:12 NASB

And we are sure of this, that He will listen to us whenever we ask Him for anything in line with His will. And if we really know He is listening when we talk to Him and make our requests, then we can be sure that He will answer us.
I John 5:14–15 TLB

Lord, today I am desperate for a place of rest. Please draw me into Your presence. Just like a little sparrow, I want to find a place and settle into a nest there—tucked away in Your presence until I can draw strength from You and face the storm again. AMEN

I long, yes, faint with longing to be able to enter Your courtyard and come near to the Living God. Even the sparrows and swallows are welcome to come and nest among Your altars and there have their young, O Lord of heaven's armies, my King and my God! How happy are those who can live in Your Temple, singing Your praises.
Psalm 84:2–4 TLB

Are not two sparrows sold for a cent? And *yet* not one of them will fall to the ground apart from your Father. But the very hairs of your head are all numbered. So do not fear; you are more valuable than many sparrows.
Matthew 10:29–31 NASB

Lord, please don't let this hard thing that I am going through become my identity. I am willing to use the ways You help me in difficult days to encourage others, but I don't want to be labeled with my problems or brokenness.

I would rather be known as someone who loves You and listens to You and trusts You—and is helped.

AMEN

See how very much our heavenly Father loves us, for He allows us to be called His children—think of it—and we really *are*! But since most people don't know God, naturally they don't understand that we are His children. Yes, dear friends, we are already God's children, right now, and we can't even imagine what it is going to be like later on. But we do know this, that when He comes we will be like Him, as a result of seeing Him as He really is.

I John 3:1–2 TLB

Those who fear You will be glad when they see me,
Because I have hoped in Your word.

Psalm 119:74 NKJV

Lord, I've heard that in conflict whoever gets to the cross first wins—so here I am! I am choosing to surrender all my accusations against others. Please replace the blame that has agitated my heart with grace, and give me the peace of love and forgiveness toward the very ones who have offended me. AMEN

Let all bitterness, wrath, anger, clamor, and evil speaking be put away from you, with all malice. And be kind to one another, tenderhearted, forgiving one another, even as God in Christ forgave you.
Ephesians 4:31–32 NKJV

Be gentle and ready to forgive; never hold grudges. Remember, the Lord forgave you, so you must forgive others.
Colossians 3:13 TLB

Most important of all, continue to show deep love for each other, for love makes up for many of your faults.
I Peter 4:8 TLB

Lord, this new set of circumstances has brought me to a place I can only call my "new normal." It is not what my heart wants or had hoped for, and I cannot make sudden peace with it. But You are already helping me through this day. I am leaning on You to help me face this new future one day at a time. AMEN

He does not fear bad news, nor live in dread of what may happen. For he is settled in his mind that Jehovah will take care of him.

Psalm 112:7 TLB

Blessed is the man who trusts in the LORD and whose trust is the LORD. For he will be like a tree planted by the water, that extends its roots by a stream and will not fear when the heat comes; but its leaves will be green, and it will not be anxious in a year of drought nor cease to yield fruit.

Jeremiah 17:7–8 NASB

I waited patiently for the LORD to help me, and He turned to me and heard my cry. He lifted me out of the pit of despair, out of the mud and the mire. He set my feet on solid ground and steadied me as I walked along. He has given me a new song to sing, a hymn of praise to our God. Many will see what He has done and be amazed. They will put their trust in the LORD.

Psalm 40:1–3 NLT

Lord, I want to shine for You—but not as a mirror reflecting a dizzying array of the thoughts and opinions around me, but as a lantern with the light of Your life within me. AMEN

Let your light shine before men in such a way
that they may see your good works,
and glorify your Father who is in heaven.
Matthew 5:16 NASB

Once more Jesus addressed the crowd. He said,
"I am the Light of the world. He who follows Me will not
walk in the darkness, but will have the Light of life."
John 8:12 AMP

I saw no temple in it, for the Lord God Almighty
[the Omnipotent, the Ruler of all] and the Lamb
are its temple. And the city has no need of the sun
nor of the moon to give light to it, for the glory
(splendor, radiance) of God has illumined it,
and the Lamb is its lamp and light.
Revelation 21:22–23 AMP

Lord, when my days are hard, I can imagine that You sit a little closer to the edge of Your throne because You want to hear what this child, whom You love so much, will say about You when she is confused and hurting.

When I am distressed, I want to say what is true about You as a gift of love and honor to You—in spite of my circumstances. It is my gift of worship. AMEN

I said to the LORD, "You are my Lord;
I have no good besides You."
Psalm 16:2 AMP

That my soul may sing praise to You and not be silent.
O LORD my God, I will give thanks to You forever.
Psalm 30:12 AMP

But as for me, I will sing of Your mighty strength *and* power; yes, I will sing joyfully of Your lovingkindness in the morning; for You have been my stronghold and a refuge in the day of my distress.
Psalm 59:16 AMP

Lord, I am praying because I need for You to hear and answer my prayer. But I realize Your Word says if I have malice or wickedness in my heart, You will not hear me. I want my heart to be clean so there is no hindrance to my prayer. What are You seeing when you look at me? Please point out anything that is grieving You so I can repent and be forgiven.

AMEN

If I had not confessed the sin in my heart,
the Lord would not have listened.
Psalm 66:18 NLT

Only those with pure hands and hearts, who do not practice dishonesty and lying. They will receive God's own goodness as their blessing from Him, planted in their lives by God Himself, their Savior.
Psalm 24:4–5 TLB

If we confess our sins, He is faithful and righteous to forgive us our sins and to cleanse us from all unrighteousness.
I John 1:9 NASB

Lord, I am so grateful that there is no need for me to ask You, "Why am I here?" You planned me, created me and wrote down my life. It is the desire of my heart to live all my days the way You planned them and wrote them down. When I stray from Your plan for me, please nudge me back into Your way. AMEN

The LORD will accomplish what concerns me;
Your lovingkindness, O LORD, is everlasting;
do not forsake the works of Your hands.
Psalm 138:8 NASB

You made all the delicate, inner parts of my body and knit me together in my mother's womb. Thank You for making me so wonderfully complex! Your workmanship is marvelous—how well I know it. You watched me as I was being formed in utter seclusion, as I was woven together in the dark of the womb. You saw me before I was born. Every day of my life was recorded in Your book. Every moment was laid out before a single day had passed.
Psalm 139:13–16 NLT

Lord, when I pray for a specific answer that I am looking for, I don't seem to hear a clear "yes" or a clear "no." So I still wonder what the answer is. But when I pray with all my heart that Your will be done, I know that when the answer comes, it will be what I prayed for. AMEN

Pray then like this "Our Father in heaven, hallowed be your name. Your kingdom come, your will be done, on earth as it is in heaven."
Matthew 6:9–10 ESV

Please listen and answer me,
for I am overwhelmed by my troubles.
Psalm 55:2 NLT

Oh, how great is Your goodness to those who publicly declare that You will rescue them. For You have stored up great blessings for those who trust and reverence You.
Psalm 31:19 TLB

Lord, my heart is open to You. You are welcome in every room to do a complete renovation. Demolish and toss out every old thing that grieves You and everything that has weighed me down. I want it to be a comfortable place for You to live. Make it obvious that You are present in my life. AMEN

And I will give you a new heart—I will give you new and right desires—and put a new spirit within you. I will take out your stony hearts of sin and give you new hearts of love.

EZEKIEL 36:26 TLB

And I pray that Christ will be more and more at home in your hearts, living within you as you trust in Him. May your roots go down deep into the soil of God's marvelous love; and may you be able to feel and understand, as all God's children should, how long, how wide, how deep, and how high His love really is; and to experience this love for yourselves, though it is so great that you will never see the end of it or fully know or understand it. And so at last you will be filled up with God Himself.

Ephesians 3:17–19 TLB

Yes, everything else is worthless when compared with the infinite value of knowing Christ Jesus my Lord. For His sake I have discarded everything else, counting it all as garbage, so that I could gain Christ.

Philippians 3:8 NLT

Lord, people like to say that their troubles have "come to pass." But my situation has not "come to pass"—it has come to stay. Aside from a miracle, my situation is not likely to change.

To look at it as my future is almost overwhelming! Please give me the grace to endure and a heart to look for Your fingerprints on every day. Bring Your gladness to my heart and help me see the beauty of my days. AMEN

Yet what we suffer now is nothing compared
to the glory He will give us later.
Romans 8:18 TLB

One thing I have asked of the LORD, and that I will seek:
That I may dwell in the house of the LORD
[in His presence] all the days of my life,
To gaze upon the beauty [the delightful loveliness
and majestic grandeur] of the LORD
And to meditate in His temple.
Psalm 27:4 AMP

Lord, I cannot hold everything in my life together and keep it from spinning out of control. Your Word says that You have the power to hold all things together, so I'm putting it all in Your hands. AMEN

He was before all else began and it is His power
that holds everything together.
Colossians 1:17 TLB

Let Him have all your worries and cares,
for He is always thinking about you
and watching everything that concerns you.
I Peter 5:7 TLB

For I am persuaded that neither death nor life, nor angels
nor principalities nor powers, nor things present
nor things to come, nor height nor depth, nor any other
created thing, shall be able to separate us from
the love of God which is in Christ Jesus our Lord.
Romans 8:38–39 NKJV

Lord, in this difficult season, I am choosing to focus on obeying You—expecting that You will use my obedience to teach me something that You want me to know. Something that I could miss if I don't obey You. Something I might otherwise never know about. AMEN

Being found in appearance as a man, He humbled Himself by becoming obedient to the point of death, even death on a cross.
Philippians 2:8 NASB

In the days of His flesh, He offered up both prayers and supplications with loud crying and tears to the One able to save Him from death, and He was heard because of His piety. Although He was a Son, He learned obedience from the things which He suffered.
Hebrews 5:7–8 NASB

We destroy arguments and every lofty opinion raised against the knowledge of God, and take every thought captive to obey Christ.
II Corinthians 10:5 ESV

Lord, I see others busy with ministries
and I wonder what ministry is my calling?
My passion? My spiritual gift?

But before I pick something and sign up and get busy,
my heart is telling me that my first calling is not
to "do" but to love You—to spend time with You
and look in Your Word for Your heart. I ask You
to choose however You want Your life to flow
through me in service and ministry. AMEN

As the deer pants for water, so I long for You, O God.
Psalm 42:1 TLB

I am the vine, you are the branches; he who abides in Me
and I in him, he bears much fruit, for apart from Me
you can do nothing.
John 15:5 NASB

O Lord, the Hope of Israel, all who turn away from you
shall be disgraced and shamed; they are registered
for earth and not for glory, for they have forsaken
the Lord, the Fountain of living waters.
Jeremiah 17:13 TLB

Lord, it seems that we are surrounded by disastrous possibilities and stories of the unthinkable every day. But I don't want to focus on that and live with a fearful heart. No matter what politics are in control, life will go on and I want You to be the Lord of mine!

Knowing that You are the Lord of all of it, I can face the scary unknown of coming days knowing that You are already there. AMEN

'Do not fear, for I am with you; Do not anxiously look about you, for I am your God. I will strengthen you, surely I will help you, surely I will uphold you with My righteous right hand.'
Isaiah 41:10 NASB

For the kingdom is the LORD's
and He rules over the nations.
Psalm 22:28 NASB

In his hand is the life of every living thing
and the breath of all mankind.
Job 12:10 ESV

Lord, I need You and I am thankful that my prayers will not expire—prayer never dies

You will not forget my need—You will remember the cry of my heart. AMEN!

But certainly God has heard; He has given heed
to the voice of my prayer.
Psalm 66:19 NASB

Mark this well: The Lord has set apart the redeemed
for Himself. Therefore He will listen to me
and answer when I call to Him.
Psalm 4:3 TLB

And as He took the scroll, the twenty-four Elders
fell down before the Lamb, each with a harp and golden
vials filled with incense—the prayers of God's people!
Revelation 5:8 TLB

Lord, I am almost overwhelmed when I think how many people are hurting around me. Make me like an old, blue blanket—always ready to wrap the comfort of kindness and prayer around a broken heart that I cannot fix. AMEN

Since you have been chosen by God who has given you this new kind of life, and because of His deep love and concern for you, you should practice tenderhearted mercy and kindness to others. Don't worry about making a good impression on them, but be ready to suffer quietly and patiently.

Colossians 3:12 TLB

What a wonderful God we have—He is the Father of our Lord Jesus Christ, the source of every mercy, and the one who so wonderfully comforts and strengthens us in our hardships and trials. And why does He do this? So that when others are troubled, needing our sympathy and encouragement, we can pass on to them this same help and comfort God has given us.

II Corinthians 1:3–4 TLB

Bear one another's burdens, and so fulfill the law of Christ.

Galatians 6:2 NKJV

Lord, I don't know what I don't know, so I don't know how to pray. I don't even know what to ask You to do. I am so thankful that You don't need to be tutored by my instruction in my prayers. With a whole heart, I ask You to move Your will from heaven to earth in this situation. AMEN

And He said unto them, "When ye pray, say, Our Father which art in heaven, Hallowed be thy name. Thy kingdom come. Thy will be done, as in heaven, so in earth."
Luke 11:2 KJV

In the same way the Spirit also helps our weakness; for we do not know how to pray as we should, but the Spirit Himself intercedes for us with groanings too deep for words; and He who searches the hearts knows what the mind of the Spirit is, because He intercedes for the saints according to the will of God.
Romans 8:26–27 NASB

Lord, there is a peace that to me is even greater than any turmoil of the day. It is the peace in my heart that comes from knowing that there is nothing wrong between You and me. You Yourself have set me free from all the distress that results from my sin. Please keep my spirit sensitive to anything that threatens to rob my peace by tempting me to put myself in charge instead of trusting You with everything. AMEN

So if the Son makes you free,
then you are unquestionably free.
John 8:36 AMP

For, dear brothers, you have been given freedom:
not freedom to do wrong, but freedom to love and serve
each other. For the whole Law can be summed up
in this one command: "Love others as you love yourself."
Galatians 5:13–14 TLB

While they were talking about this, Jesus Himself
[suddenly] stood among them and said to them,
"Peace be to you."
Luke 24:36 AMP

Lord, as I count my blessings in my walk with You, it is not the memories of a fresh new house or the joy of a special trip that bring the most joy. It is remembering the hard places where I have seen Your work in my heart—the changes you made that have been permanent and became tools for me to share comfort with others. These are the treasures in my life. AMEN

We can rejoice, too, when we run into problems and trials, for we know that they are good for us—they help us learn to be patient. And patience develops strength of character in us and helps us trust God more each time we use it until finally our hope and faith are strong and steady. Then, when that happens, we are able to hold our heads high no matter what happens and know that all is well, for we know how dearly God loves us, and we feel this warm love everywhere within us because God has given us the Holy Spirit to fill our hearts with His love.

Romans 5:3–5 TLB

Dear brothers, is your life full of difficulties and temptations? Then be happy, for when the way is rough, your patience has a chance to grow. So let it grow, and don't try to squirm out of your problems. For when your patience is finally in full bloom, then you will be ready for anything, strong in character, full and complete. If you want to know what God wants you to do, ask Him, and He will gladly tell you, for He is always ready to give a bountiful supply of wisdom to all who ask Him; He will not resent it.

James 1:2–5 TLB

Lord, I am trying to trust You completely, but everything is in such a mess I keep thinking I need to DO something! Help me to understand that You are Lord over everything—including this mess—and let go and trust You. Right now—I choose to declare that You are Lord over this! AMEN

Don't worry about anything; instead, pray about everything; tell God your needs, and don't forget to thank Him for His answers. If you do this, you will experience God's peace, which is far more wonderful than the human mind can understand. His peace will keep your thoughts and your hearts quiet and at rest as you trust in Christ Jesus.
Philippians 4:6–7 TLB

Trust in the Lord with all your heart, and lean not on your own understanding; in all your ways acknowledge Him, and He shall direct your paths.
Proverbs 3:5–6 NKJV

Lord, I hear myself saying to You, *I need, I need, I need.* But I am realizing that what I need is to stop approaching You as a vending machine that dispenses my selections. My real need is to simply let You use my needs to show me how You want to work in my life. AMEN

The things you have learned and received and heard
and seen in me, practice these things,
and the God of peace will be with you.
Philippians 4:9 NASB

But seek first His kingdom and His righteousness,
and all these things will be added to you.
Matthew 6:33 NASB

Now to Him who is able to do far more abundantly beyond all that we ask or think, according to the power that works within us, to Him *be* the glory in the church and in Christ Jesus to all generations forever and ever. Amen.
Ephesians 3:20–21 NASB

Lord, how can I pray for my friend? What is it that You are wanting to do for her? Please pull my heart toward the comforting words You want me to give her. Give me Scriptures that show me how to pray for her. Please make a path for her out of her personal nightmare. AMEN

The eyes of the LORD are toward the righteous and His ears are *open* to their cry. The face of the LORD is against evildoers, to cut off the memory of them from the earth. *The righteous* cry, and the LORD hears and delivers them out of all their troubles. The LORD is near to the brokenhearted and saves those who are crushed in spirit.
Psalm 34:15–18 NASB

Be to me a great protecting Rock, where I am always welcome, safe from all attacks. For You have issued the order to save me.
Psalm 71:3 TLB

God *is* our refuge and strength, a very present help in trouble.
Psalm 46:1 NKJV

Lord, I keep trying to imagine how You are going to work out this problem—and I always guess wrong. But when I look at the hummingbird outside my window, and I think about how You designed his tiny, intricate feathers and his little beating heart, and I consider how You have equipped him to fly almost unbelievable distances, and then labeled him with a touch of Your beauty—I know you've got this. AMEN

For all God's words are right, and everything He does
is worthy of our trust.
Psalm 33:4 TLB

For You are great and do wondrous deeds;
You alone are God.
Psalm 86:10 NASB

The Lord is my rock, my fortress, and my Savior;
my God is my rock, in whom I find protection.
He is my shield, the power that saves me,
and my place of safety.
Psalm 18:2 NLT

Lord, I need to care more about the lost than I really do. There are days when I forget their urgent need. The magnitude of the broken lives around me has dulled my heart. Show me one, Lord, that You want me to focus my prayers on. Speak to my heart the ways You want me to be Your hands and heart to them. I can start with one. AMEN

What man of you, having a hundred sheep, if he has lost one of them, does not leave the ninety-nine in the open country, and go after the one that is lost, until he finds it?
Luke 15:4 ESV

Jesus said to him, "I am the way, the truth, and the life. No one comes to the Father except through Me."
John 14:6 NKJV

Quietly trust yourself to Christ your Lord, and if anybody asks why you believe as you do, be ready to tell him, and do it in a gentle and respectful way.
I Peter 3:15 TLB

Lord, I am trusting You that this season that seems so dull and disheartening will turn out to be a new beginning for me. A fresh season of understanding Your faithfulness in a deeper way. AMEN

But forget all that—it is nothing compared to what I'm going to do! For I'm going to do a brand new thing. See, I have already begun! Don't you see it? I will make a road through the wilderness of the world for My people to go home, and create rivers for them in the desert!
Isaiah 43:18–19 TLB

Everything is appropriate in its own time. But though God has planted eternity in the hearts of men, even so, many cannot see the whole scope of God's work from beginning to end.
Ecclesiastes 3:11 TLB

No, dear brothers, I am still not all I should be, but I am bringing all my energies to bear on this one thing: Forgetting the past and looking forward to what lies ahead, I strain to reach the end of the race and receive the prize for which God is calling us up to heaven because of what Christ Jesus did for us.
Philippians 3:13–14 TLB

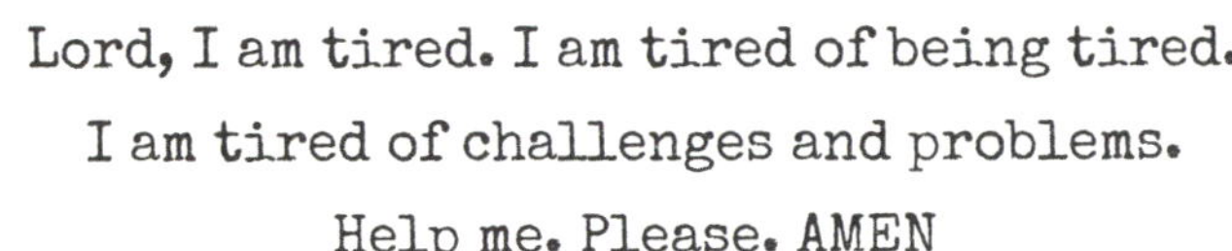
Lord, I am tired. I am tired of being tired.
I am tired of challenges and problems.
Help me. Please. AMEN

I am poor and weak, yet the Lord is thinking about me right now! O my God, You are my helper. You are my Savior; come quickly, and save me. Please don't delay!
Psalm 40:17 TLB

The Lord hears His people when they call to Him for help. He rescues them from all their troubles.
Psalm 34:17 NLT

Come to Me, all who are weary and heavy-laden, and I will give you rest.
Matthew 11:28 NASB

Lord, I don't have to tell You that I pretty much just want my own way—in pretty much everything. But Your word has told me that my thoughts are not Your thoughts and Your ways are higher than mine.

It is really hard for me to surrender to Your ways, but right now, my heart is kneeling and saying "not my way, but Yours. Not my will, but Yours." AMEN

"For My thoughts are not your thoughts,
nor are your ways My ways," declares the LORD.
"For as the heavens are higher than the earth,
so are My ways higher than your ways
and My thoughts than your thoughts.
Isaiah 55:8–9 NASB

Make me know Your ways, O LORD;
Teach me Your paths.
Psalm 25:4 NASB

He will teach the ways that are right and best
to those who humbly turn to Him.
Psalm 25:9 TLB

Lord, I have been so disappointed in this situation. You didn't do what I thought You should do. And in my disappointment, I have pulled away from supportive praying and from having an encouraging heart.

Please forgive me. I will start again to pray and try to trust Your wisdom and timing.

AMEN

Wait patiently for the LORD. Be brave and courageous.
Yes, wait patiently for the LORD.
Psalm 27:14 NLT

I wait for the LORD, my soul does wait,
and in His word do I hope.
Psalm 130:5 NASB

Lord, just when I think I have sifted all the trash out of my heart, out of the blue an old grudge comes floating up. Like an old rotten tomato that was forgotten in the back of my fridge.

Lord, I gladly forgive this person! I don't want the heaviness of unforgiveness in my heart. Please forgive me, too, and restore me to my peace. Thank You for healing and cleansing this memory.

AMEN

For I will be merciful to their unrighteousness,
and their sins and their lawless deeds
I will remember no more.
Hebrews 8:12 NKJV

I, even I, am He who blots out your transgressions
for My own sake; And I will not remember your sins.
Isaiah 43:25 NKJV

Do not remember the sins of my youth or my
transgressions; According to Your lovingkindness
remember me, For Your goodness' sake, O Lord.
Psalm 25:7 NASB

Lord, I want to have a faithful heart that You can count on. A steadfast heart that is willing to be taught and willing to obey day in and day out. Your love for me is changeless today and tomorrow. I want to be constant in loving You today and tomorrow. AMEN

Let us hold fast the confession of our hope without wavering, for He who promised is faithful.
Hebrews 10:23 NKJV

So, my dear brothers and sisters, be strong and immovable. Always work enthusiastically for the Lord, for you know that nothing you do for the Lord is ever useless.
I Corinthians 15:58 NLT

May the Lord lead your hearts into a full understanding and expression of the love of God and the patient endurance that comes from Christ.
II Thessalonians 3:5 NLT

Lord, I have confessed my sin. Wash me.
Wash away not only the sin itself, but the sadness
and the ugly memory it has left me with.
Please heal the damage to my own heart. Restore me
to a clean and open conscience—the joy of being
just as if I had never sinned. AMEN

Wash me clean from my guilt. Purify me from my sin.
Psalm 51:2 NLT

Create in me a new, clean heart, O God,
filled with clean thoughts and right desires.
Psalm 51:10 TLB

He renews my strength. He guides me along
right paths, bringing honor to His name.
Psalm 23:3 NLT

Lord, I gladly submit myself to Your lordship over everything in my life. I used to think that only meant that I would obey You. But now I see it is much more. When I live in Your lordship, you have the right and wisdom to move the pieces of my life around without asking me while You hold me securely and give me the very best care and results. I am so grateful for the freedom and security I have in You—for working for me in what You see that I can't see. AMEN

Yet for us there is but one God, the Father, from whom are all things and we exist for Him; and one Lord, Jesus Christ, by whom are all things, and we exist through Him.
I Corinthians 8:6 NASB

You see, we don't go around preaching about ourselves. We preach that Jesus Christ is Lord, and we ourselves are Your servants for Jesus' sake.
II Corinthians 4:5 NLT

Delight yourself in the Lord; and He will give you the desires of your heart. Commit your way to the Lord, trust also in Him, and He will do it.
Psalm 37:4–5 NASB

Lord, You are the only hope for the broken lives I see. Lives that would be so different if they only knew You. Because You sought me out and changed my life, I know that you can change them, too—and that You want to.

Lord, invade their dreams with the reality of Your existence. Invade their thoughts with Your truth. Invade their hearts with hope for their brokenness. Reveal Yourself and let your mercy and love overwhelm their chaos. AMEN

No one can come to Me unless the Father who sent Me draws him; and I will raise him up at the last day.
John 6:44 NKJV

For God did not send His Son into the world to condemn the world, but that the world through Him might be saved.
John 3:17 NKJV

And this is eternal life, that they may know You, the only true God, and Jesus Christ whom You have sent.
John 17:3 NKJV

Lord, please give me an attentive heart so that I can hear You when You speak to me. Guard my mind and protect me from confusing Your words and directions to me with my own thoughts. Don't let my heart wander from Scripture. AMEN

My sheep hear My voice, and I know them,
and they follow Me.
John 10:27 NASB

Call to Me and I will answer you, and I will tell you
great and mighty things, which you do not know.
Jeremiah 33:3 NASB

So faith comes from hearing,
and hearing by the word of Christ.
Romans 10:17 NASB

Lord, how do I pray when I know that this situation is not going to end well? In this storm that will not end without loss, I ask You to be my strength in all my weakness and helplessness. AMEN

He has said to me, "My grace is sufficient for You [My lovingkindness and My mercy are more than enough—always available—regardless of the situation]; for [My] power is being perfected [and is completed and shows itself most effectively] in [your] weakness." Therefore, I will all the more gladly boast in my weaknesses, so that the power of Christ [may completely enfold me and] may dwell in me.
II Corinthians 12:9 AMP

Seek the LORD and His strength;
Seek His face continually.
I Chronicles 16:11 NASB

Then He said to them, "Go your way, eat the fat, drink the sweet, and send portions to those for whom nothing is prepared; for *this* day *is* holy to our Lord. Do not sorrow, for the joy of the LORD is your strength."
Nehemiah 8:10 NKJV

Lord, You have given me a will—a free will—that I might choose to belong to You. You bore not only my sins but also my wicked nature on the cross so that I can be truly free from sin. Not just free from my past, but free from being controlled by my sin in the future! I don't have the words to describe my thankfulness, but all of me bows with gratitude. You have filled my future with the bright hope that is You. AMEN

All honor to God, the God and Father of our Lord Jesus Christ; for it is His boundless mercy that has given us the privilege of being born again so that we are now members of God's own family. Now we live in the hope of eternal life because Christ rose again from the dead.
I Peter 1:3 TLB

And now, just as you accepted Christ Jesus as your Lord, you must continue to follow Him. Let your roots grow down into Him, and let your lives be built on Him. Then your faith will grow strong in the truth you were taught, and you will overflow with thankfulness.
Colossians 2:6 –7 NLT

If you acknowledge *and* confess with your mouth that Jesus is Lord [recognizing His power, authority, and majesty as God], and believe in your heart that God raised Him from the dead, you will be saved.
Romans 10:9 AMP

Lord, I can't control much of anything that is going on around me but I can still make choices. And I choose to trust Your character and Your Word and Your love for me. I choose to obey You and I choose to keep my heart surrendered to You. AMEN

For this reason I also suffer these things, but I am not ashamed; for I know whom I have believed and I am convinced that He is able to guard what I have entrusted to Him until that day.
II Timothy 1:12 NASB

If you love Me, obey My commandments.
John 14:15 NLT

For to me, to live is Christ and to die is gain.
Philippians 1:21 NASB

Lord, I know that I need to surrender everything to You. It is so easy to sing "All to Jesus I Surrender" but how can I do that? "All"—What is all? What is everything in my situation? "to Jesus"—You are the only one I can trust with this. "Surrender"—How do I give it up and not take it back?

I open my hands and lift them up to You—please take everything I'm struggling to surrender. AMEN

Therefore I urge you, brethren, by the mercies of God, to present your bodies a living and holy sacrifice, acceptable to God, which is your spiritual service of worship.
Romans 12:1 NASB

I have been crucified with Christ; it is no longer I who live, but Christ lives in me; and the life which I now live in the flesh I live by faith in the Son of God, who loved me and gave Himself for me.
Galatians 2:20 NKJV

For whoever desires to save his life will lose it, but whoever loses his life for My sake will save it.
Luke 9:24 NKJV

Lord, help me to "tune my heart to sing Thy praise!" That old hymn calls to me to use my heart as an instrument to praise You—letting go of every distraction that is not "in tune" with You. You are worthy to receive all praise and honor!

As a continual act of worship—I want to live my life in harmony with who You are. AMEN

The Lord is my strength and song,
and He has become my salvation.
Psalm 118:14 NASB

To whom God willed to make known what is the riches of the glory of this mystery among the Gentiles, which is Christ in you, the hope of glory.
Colossians 1:27 NASB

Remain in Me, and I will remain in you. For a branch cannot produce fruit if it is severed from the vine, and you cannot be fruitful unless you remain in Me. Yes, I am the vine; you are the branches. Those who remain in Me, and I in them, will produce much fruit. For apart from Me you can do nothing.
John 15:4–5 NLT

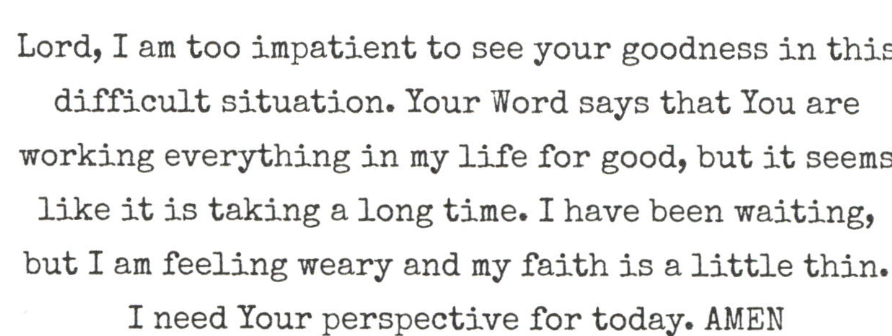

Lord, I am too impatient to see your goodness in this difficult situation. Your Word says that You are working everything in my life for good, but it seems like it is taking a long time. I have been waiting, but I am feeling weary and my faith is a little thin. I need Your perspective for today. AMEN

Now faith is the assurance of things hoped for,
the conviction of things not seen.
Hebrews 11:1 NASB

And now, Lord, for what do I wait?
Psalm 39:7 NASB

For I have given rest to the weary
and joy to the sorrowing.
Jeremiah 31:25 NLT

Lord, my words have no power or influence on this person I am praying for—but Yours do. Please make Yourself known in their life and invade the darkness of their heart with the light of who You are and the power of Your love. AMEN

Therefore He is also able to save to the uttermost
those who come to God through Him,
since He always lives to make intercession for them.
Hebrews 7:25 NKJV

Then they will come to their senses and escape from
Satan's trap of slavery to sin, which he uses
to catch them whenever he likes, and then they
can begin doing the will of God.
II Timothy 2:26 TLB

The Son of Man has come to seek
and to save that which was lost.
Luke 19:10 NKJV

Lord, I want to be someone You can trust. I don't want to miss anything in my life that You wanted to give me—but couldn't trust me with because of my pride or my preoccupation with my own agenda or because I haven't trusted You. Please show me anything in my heart that is a road block to the wonderful plans You have waiting for me. AMEN

"For I know the plans I have for you," says the Lord.
"They are plans for good and not for evil,
to give you a future and a hope."
Jeremiah 29:11 TLB

And now may the God of peace, who brought again from the dead our Lord Jesus, equip you with all you need for doing His will. May He who became the great Shepherd of the sheep by an everlasting agreement between God and you, signed with His blood, produce in you through the power of Christ all that is pleasing to Him. To Him be glory forever and ever. Amen.
Hebrews 13:20–21 TLB

And I am certain that God, who began the good work within you, will continue His work until it is finally finished on the day when Christ Jesus returns.
Philippians 1:6 NLT

Lord, You know how it feels to be innocent and rejected and falsely accused. You haven't told me how to pray for myself when I have been betrayed by a friend. You've only told me to love my enemies and pray for those who hurt me and mistreat me. So, Lord, I ask You to pour out Your love and all the good You want to do for the one who hurt me. And please use those prayers to heal my heart. AMEN

You have heard the law that says, "Love your neighbor and hate your enemy." But I say, love your enemies! Pray for those who persecute you! In that way, you will be acting as true children of your Father in heaven. For He gives His sunlight to both the evil and the good, and He sends rain on the just and the unjust alike. If you love only those who love you, what reward is there for that? Even corrupt tax collectors do that much. If you are kind only to your friends, how are you different from anyone else? Even pagans do that. But you are to be perfect, even as your Father in heaven is perfect.

Matthew 5:43–48 NLT

But to you who are willing to listen, I say, love your enemies! Do good to those who hate you. Bless those who curse you. Pray for those who hurt you.

Luke 6:27–28 NLT

Lord, on Ash Wednesday I saw a man with an ashen cross of repentance on his forehead. It caused me to ask myself: *Am I living daily with the cross in my heart—so that my selfishness is continually put to death?* Without that kind of surrender, the power of Your life shining forth in me and drawing others to You will be hindered. AMEN

Don't you see how wonderfully kind, tolerant, and patient God is with you? Does this mean nothing to you? Can't you see that His kindness is intended to turn you from your sin?
Romans 2:4 NLT

But I confess my sins; I am deeply sorry for what I have done.
Psalm 38:18 NLT

Seek the LORD while you can find Him. Call on Him now while He is near. Let the wicked change their ways and banish the very thought of doing wrong. Let them turn to the LORD that He may have mercy on them. Yes, turn to our God, for He will forgive generously.
Isaiah 55:6–7 NLT

Lord, I humble myself before you—
choosing not to be offended or dismayed
by whatever you allow in my life.
Your character is above all these circumstances.
And Your love for me is unchanging. AMEN

Give thanks to the God of heaven,
For His lovingkindness is everlasting.
Psalm 136:26 NASB

And He gives grace generously. As the Scriptures say,
"God opposes the proud but gives grace to the humble."
James 4:6 NLT

As for God, His way is blameless;
The word of the Lord is tried;
He is a shield to all who take refuge in Him.
Psalm 18:30 NASB

Lord, I believe I mostly know all the "rights" to do and "wrongs" not to do, but I want to know Your heart in a deeper way. Through Your word, day by day, please show me what pleases You and help me see what grieves Your heart so that I may not only love You more, but also walk more carefully before You. AMEN

Don't cause the Holy Spirit sorrow by the way you live. Remember, He is the one who marks you to be present on that day when salvation from sin will be complete.

Ephesians 4:30 TLB

For though once your heart was full of darkness, now it is full of light from the Lord, and your behavior should show it! Because of this light within you, you should do only what is good and right and true. Learn as you go along what pleases the Lord.

Ephesians 5:8–10 TLB

My prayer for you is that you will overflow more and more with love for others, and at the same time keep on growing in spiritual knowledge and insight, for I want you always to see clearly the difference between right and wrong, and to be inwardly clean, no one being able to criticize you from now until our Lord returns.

Philippians 1:9–10 TLB

Lord, help me get over myself! While I keep talking to You about myself there are other people I need to notice and care about. Turn the attention of my heart toward being a blessing to someone else today. Would you pick someone who needs encouragement and put them on my radar today? Then, would You show me how to bless them? AMEN

For God is not unfair. How can He forget your hard work for Him, or forget the way you used to show your love for Him—and still do—by helping His children?
Hebrews 6:10 TLB

For even the Son of Man did not come to be served, but to serve, and to give His life a ransom for many.
Mark 10:45 NKJV

God has given each of you some special abilities; be sure to use them to help each other, passing on to others God's many kinds of blessings.
I Peter 4:10 TLB

Lord, You and I both know that sometimes when I am talking to someone, there is an unkind thought or rebuke or complaint tumbling around in my mind—like a dirty sock in a dryer. And, before I know it, it just tumbles out! Staining the air—and ears.

No matter how hard I try to look lovelier on the outside, my rogue tongue can spoil the whole effect with ugliness. I need beauty in my mouth! Please guard my mouth and supply me with either the beauty of Your words and heart or the gift of silence. AMEN

Help me, Lord, to keep my mouth shut
and my lips sealed.
Psalm 141:3 TLB

Watch your tongue and keep your mouth shut,
and you will stay out of trouble.
Proverbs 21:23 NLT

Kind words are like honey—sweet to the soul
and healthy for the body.
Proverbs 16:24 NLT

Lord, in the turmoil of these days
and the gathering darkness, shelter me
in the light of Your presence. AMEN

For You light my lamp;
The LORD my God illumines my darkness.
Psalm 18:28 NASB

How blessed are the people who know the joyful sound!
O LORD, they walk in the light of Your countenance.
Psalm 89:15 NASB

Then Jesus again spoke to them, saying, "I am the Light
of the world; he who follows Me will not walk
in the darkness, but will have the Light of life."
John 8:12 NASB

Lord, even though others know about this painful time in my life, I am trying to look "okay" to them. But, on the inside, where no one else can see but You, I am sobbing. You understand my tearless grief. Let Your praises inhabit my heart and keep my mind steady as I trust You to comfort and restore me in ways I cannot yet see. AMEN

He heals the brokenhearted and binds up their wounds.
Psalm 147:3 NKJV

Blessed are those who mourn,
for they shall be comforted.
Matthew 5:4 NKJV

Because the Lord is my Shepherd,
I have everything I need!
Psalm 23:1 TLB

Lord, as a child I sang, "I am weak but You are strong." And now I know how very true that is. I am weak and I really need Your strength. AMEN

But they that wait upon the Lord shall renew their strength. They shall mount up with wings like eagles; they shall run and not be weary; they shall walk and not faint.

Isaiah 40:31 TLB

Last of all I want to remind you that your strength must come from the Lord's mighty power within you.

Ephesians 6:10 TLB

He gives strength to the weary, and to him who has no might He increases power.

Isaiah 40:29 AMP

Lord, I live in the midst of Your goodness to me—within and without. Within—I have life, health and salvation. Without—I am surrounded by beauty, provision and safety. You, Lord, are completely good. AMEN

The LORD is good to all, and His mercies are over all His works.
Psalm 145:9 NASB

O give thanks to the LORD, for He is good; For His lovingkindness is everlasting.
I Chronicles 16:34 NASB

For the LORD God is a sun and shield; the LORD will give grace and glory; No good thing will He withhold from those who walk uprightly.
Psalm 84:11 NKJV

Lord, my world is missing Your glory. I want to know Your glory. Not so I can have an experience to tell my friends about that will make me seem so very spiritual. But because all glory belongs to You and Your glory is part of knowing You. Please give me the gift of a burning thirst for Your presence. AMEN

He is the radiance of the glory of God and the exact imprint of his nature, and he upholds the universe by the word of his power. After making purification for sins, he sat down at the right hand of the Majesty on high.
Hebrews 1:3 ESV

And the Word became flesh and dwelt among us, and we beheld His glory, the glory as of the only begotten of the Father, full of grace and truth.
John 1:14 NKJV

But we all, with unveiled face, beholding as in a mirror the glory of the Lord, are being transformed into the same image from glory to glory, just as from the Lord, the Spirit.
II Corinthians 3:18 NASB

Lord, I am sorry for all the ways I have hurt Your heart and missed relationship opportunities with others because I didn't know how to be a humble person. I knew not to brag or be boastful or try to be the center of attention, but until now, I didn't know what humility was. I didn't know that it is being "other oriented." It's not about my wondering what others think of me—it's about my thinking of them instead of myself. This is the decision I have to make: do I want everything to be about me—or do I want it to be about You. And You are always oriented toward others. Please make this change in me. I want everything to be about You. AMEN

Do nothing from selfishness or empty conceit, but with humility of mind regard one another as more important than yourselves.
Philippians 2:3 NASB

With all humility and gentleness, with patience, showing tolerance for one another in love.
Ephesians 4:2 NASB

Have this attitude in yourselves which was also in Christ Jesus, who, although He existed in the form of God, did not regard equality with God a thing to be grasped, but emptied Himself, taking the form of a bond-servant, and being made in the likeness of men.
Philippians 2:5–7 NASB

Lord, before I let this new problem discourage me, help me to own the truth that every kind of trouble or problem that comes into my life is an opportunity. It is an opportunity to know You better and to trust You to take advantage of it for me. You never waste anything and You won't waste this. Only You can make it worth what I am going through. AMEN

Because he has loved Me, therefore I will deliver him; I will set him securely on high, because he has known My name. He will call upon Me, and I will answer him; I will be with him in trouble; I will rescue him and honor him.

Psalm 91:14–15 NASB

For we do not have a high priest who cannot sympathize with our weaknesses, but One who has been tempted in all things as *we are, yet* without sin. Therefore let us draw near with confidence to the throne of grace, so that we may receive mercy and find grace to help in time of need.

Hebrews 4:15–16 NASB

Let Your hand be ready to help me, for I have chosen Your precepts.

Psalm 119:173 AMP

Lord, when I pray, I am tempted to start designing the way I want You to bring this person to You—giving You directions and instructions about how You could make it happen. Forgive me, Lord for not asking You how You want me to pray. You already have unfulfilled plans for this one. You know how to do what You want to do. So, I am asking You to move Your will into his reality. AMEN

The Lord is not slow about His promise, as some count slowness, but is patient toward you, not wishing for any to perish but for all to come to repentance.
II Peter 3:9 NASB

For all have sinned and fall short of the glory of God.
Romans 3:23 NASB

For I am not ashamed of the gospel of Christ, for it is the power of God to salvation for everyone who believes, for the Jew first and also for the Greek.
Romans 1:16 NKJV

Lord, thank You for the peace of this day.
The peace that cleansing my heart gives me with You.
The peace that humility gives me with others.
The peace that You are Lord over my circumstances
and caring for me personally. AMEN

You keep him in perfect peace whose mind is stayed
on you, because he trusts in you.
Isaiah 26:3 ESV

Let the peace of heart that comes from Christ
be always present in your hearts and lives,
for this is your responsibility and privilege as members
of His body. And always be thankful.
Colossians 3:15 TLB

I have told you all this so that you may have peace in Me.
Here on earth you will have many trials and sorrows.
But take heart, because I have overcome the world.
John 16:33 NLT

Lord, help me to remember not to use the situation
I face as an excuse for speaking recklessly
and reacting unkindly but rather as an opportunity
to please You with clean hands, a pure heart,
and gentle words. AMEN

Make the most of your chances to tell others the Good News. Be wise in all your contacts with them. Let your conversation be gracious as well as sensible, for then you will have the right answer for everyone.
Colossians 4:5–6 TLB

Don't use bad language. Say only what is good and helpful to those you are talking to, and what will give them a blessing.
Ephesians 4:29 TLB

Create in me a new, clean heart, O God, filled with clean thoughts and right desires.
Psalm 51:10 TLB

Lord, the offenses against me are so hurtful
and heavy—too heavy for me to carry.
I have to forgive so that I can go forward.

Let those offenses be recorded in my heart
and in my mind with invisible ink—
recorded because they did happen but leaving
no bitter imprint on my life. Let them fade
with the gift of forgetting. AMEN

Love prospers when a fault is forgiven,
but dwelling on it separates close friends.
Proverbs 17:9 NLT

Above all, have fervent *and* unfailing love
for one another, because love covers
a multitude of sins [it overlooks unkindness
and unselfishly seeks the best for others].
I Peter 4:8 AMP

For if you forgive other people when they sin
against you, your heavenly Father will also forgive you.
But if you do not forgive others their sins,
your Father will not forgive your sins.
Matthew 6:14–15 NIV

Lord, I am struggling to feel hopeful. It seems that every time I think I'm going to get through this, there is a new hurdle to get over. A good ending seems further and further away. Would You sustain me today with Your Word? Only You can lift my heart with hope for better days. AMEN

Why are you in despair, O my soul? Why have you become restless *and* disquieted within me? Hope in God *and* wait expectantly for Him, for I shall yet praise Him, The help of my countenance and my God.

Psalm 42:11 AMP

But blessed are those who trust in the LORD and have made the LORD their hope and confidence.

Jeremiah 17:7 NLT

Such hope [in God's promises] never disappoints *us*, because God's love has been abundantly poured out within our hearts through the Holy Spirit who was given to us.

Romans 5:5 AMP

Lord, it does not come naturally to me to have the heart of a servant. I tend to think of my own needs first. Would You please give me Your servant's heart and teach me to pay attention to what pleases You? Alert me to the ways I can serve You first and then learn to serve others with a joyful and contented spirit. AMEN

If anyone serves Me, he must [continue to faithfully] follow Me [without hesitation, holding steadfastly to Me, conforming to My example in living and, if need be, suffering or perhaps dying because of faith in Me]; and wherever I am [in heaven's glory], there will My servant be also. If anyone serves Me, the Father will honor him.

John 12:26 AMP

Who is more important, the one who sits at the table or the one who serves? The one who sits at the table, of course. But not here! For I am among you as one who serves.

Luke 22:27 NLT

Lord, could it be that those dreaded words,
"I am wrong," could drain all the energy
out of the storm I am in? If this is what is needed,
I am willing for You to show me where I am wrong
so I can confess it with a convinced heart
and ask for forgiveness. AMEN

Confess your sins to each other and pray
for each other so that you may be healed.
The earnest prayer of a righteous person
has great power and produces wonderful results.
James 5:16 NLT

But I confess my sins;
I am deeply sorry for what I have done.
Psalm 38:18 NLT

People who conceal their sins will not prosper,
but if they confess and turn from them,
they will receive mercy.
Proverbs 28:13 NLT

Lord, Your word says that when the pot was spoiled,
the potter made it into something else.
This part of my life seems spoiled—
certainly not lived as You intended.

I am crawling up on Your potter's wheel
to just rest while You make everything
in my heart new—and remake the old into
a more joyful future that pleases You. AMEN

And yet, O Lord, You are our Father. We are the clay and You are the Potter. We are all formed by Your hand.
Isaiah 64:8 TLB

Here is another message to Jeremiah from the Lord: "Go down to the shop where clay pots and jars are made, and I will talk to you there. I did as He told me and found the potter working at his wheel. But the jar that he was forming didn't turn out as he wished, so he kneaded it into a lump and started again. Then the Lord said: O Israel, can't I do to you as this potter has done to his clay? As the clay is in the potter's hand, so are you in My hand.
Jeremiah 18:1–6 TLB

Lord, I want the gift of hunger—the kind of spiritual hunger that will never be completely satisfied until I see You. Give me the kind of hunger that drives me to Your Word—and away from spiritual "junk food" that only tickles my emotions. The kind that never lets me wander far from prayer. I don't just ask this for myself, but for all people. I am convinced that only hunger for You will meet our needs. Please have mercy in these desperate times and bless us with true hunger. AMEN

When You said, "Seek My face [in prayer,
require My presence as your greatest need],"
my heart said to You, "Your face, O Lord, I will seek
[on the authority of Your word]."
Psalm 27:8 AMP

O God, You are my God; Early will I seek You;
My soul thirsts for You; My flesh longs for You
in a dry and thirsty land where there is no water.
Psalm 63:1 NKJV

And Jesus said to them, "I am the bread of life.
He who comes to Me shall never hunger,
and he who believes in Me shall never thirst."
John 6:35 NKJV

Lord, I am noticing that my prayers in recent storms are different. They are still prayers prompted by a storm of need, but they are not prayers of panic because I have become more acquainted with your character through Your Word. What I am learning about You in Your Word has a steadying comfort.
AMEN

Whoever dwells in the shelter of the Most High will rest in the shadow of the Almighty. I will say of the LORD, "He is my refuge and my fortress, my God, in whom I trust."
Psalm 91:1–2 NIV

But I trust in Your unfailing love. I will rejoice because You have rescued me. I will sing to the LORD because He is good to me.
Psalm 13:5–6 NLT

For I am about to do something new.
See, I have already begun! Do you not see it?
I will make a pathway through the wilderness.
I will create rivers in the dry wasteland.
Isaiah 43:19 NLT

Lord, Your Word says that You love me so much that the sacrifice of Your Son for my sake was a sweet fragrance to You. It is hard for me to contemplate that kind of love. But I ask You to fill me with Your love so that I can be the sweet fragrance of Christ to those around me. AMEN

Therefore become imitators of God [copy Him and follow His example], as well-beloved children [imitate their father]; and walk *continually* in love [that is, value one another—practice empathy and compassion, unselfishly seeking the best for others], just as Christ also loved you and gave Himself up for us, an offering and sacrifice to God [slain for you, so that it became] a sweet fragrance.
Ephesians 5:1–2 AMP

But thanks be to God, who always leads us in triumph in Christ, and manifests through us the sweet aroma of the knowledge of Him in every place. For we are a fragrance of Christ to God among those who are being saved and among those who are perishing.
II Corinthians 2:14–15 NASB

Lord, even on my best days, it feels like my own personal ability to love—and keep loving—is just not adequate. It is only Your love in me that can believe the best of every person. It is the power of Your love that can endure everything without giving up. Please make me an expression of that kind of love—especially to those who are hard, really hard, to love. AMEN

Love endures with patience and serenity, love is kind and thoughtful, and is not jealous or envious; love does not brag and is not proud or arrogant. It is not rude; it is not self-seeking, it is not provoked [nor overly sensitive and easily angered]; it does not take into account a wrong endured. It does not rejoice at injustice, but rejoices with the truth [when right and truth prevail]. Love bears all things [regardless of what comes], believes all things [looking for the best in each one], hopes all things [remaining steadfast during difficult times], endures all things [without weakening].

I Corinthians 13:4–7 AMP

Lord, in this darkness, please connect me to others who are faithful "Light holders," that together we might find the courage to hold forth the beauty and power of Your life to all those the darkness has blinded. AMEN

His life is the light that shines through the darkness—and the darkness can never extinguish it.
John 1:5 TLB

But you are not like that, for you have been chosen by God Himself—you are priests of the King, you are holy and pure, you are God's very own—all this so that you may show to others how God called you out of the darkness into His wonderful light.
I Peter 2:9 TLB

Jesus shouted to the crowds, "If you trust Me, you are trusting not only Me, but also God who sent Me. For when you see Me, you are seeing the One who sent Me. I have come as a light to shine in this dark world, so that all who put their trust in Me will no longer remain in the dark.
John 12:44–46 NLT

Lord, I am back to this thing about surrender
and it is hard. Really hard. I keep taking back
what I have surrendered to You. I don't think
I'm really willing to give complete control
of my life to You and I don't know how
to make myself willing. But, I am willing
for You to make me willing. AMEN

For God is working in you, giving you the desire
and the power to do what pleases Him.
Philippians 2:13 NLT

Don't you realize that your body is the temple
of the Holy Spirit, who lives in you
and was given to you by God?
You do not belong to yourself.
I Corinthians 6:19 NLT

Lord, Your Word promises that Your mercies
are new every morning. This morning
I really need a new dose of mercy. AMEN

The faithful love of the LORD never ends!
His mercies never cease. Great is His faithfulness;
His mercies begin afresh each morning.
Lamentations 3:22–23 NLT

Surely goodness and mercy shall follow me
all the days of my life; And I will dwell
in the house of the LORD forever.
Psalm 23:6 NKJV

LORD, don't hold back Your tender mercies from me.
Let Your unfailing love and faithfulness always protect me.
Psalm 40:11 NLT

Lord, lately I feel like the invisible glue with the thankless job of trying to hold everything together—at home, at work, and at church. But that is an attitude that I don't want to encourage in myself. I can never really be invisible because I know You see me. I can never be ignored because You always hear me. And I can never be forgotten because You always remember. You are what holds my life together. AMEN

He remembered us in our weakness.
His faithful love endures forever.
Psalm 136:23 NLT

Mark this well: The Lord has set apart the redeemed for Himself. Therefore He will listen to me and answer when I call to Him.
Psalm 4:3 TLB

But in my distress I cried out to the LORD; yes, I prayed to my God for help. He heard me from His sanctuary; my cry to Him reached His ears.
Psalm 18:6 NLT

Lord, give me this day to endure the sadness in my heart. Moment by moment, let me be aware of Your presence. Day by day, help me to remember Your understanding of pain, grief, and sadness and to consider Your great love for me. AMEN

I am leaving you with a gift—peace of mind and heart! And the peace I give isn't fragile like the peace the world gives. So don't be troubled or afraid.
John 14:27 TLB

What a wonderful God we have—He is the Father of our Lord Jesus Christ, the source of every mercy, and the one who so wonderfully comforts and strengthens us in our hardships and trials. And why does He do this? So that when others are troubled, needing our sympathy and encouragement, we can pass on to them this same help and comfort God has given us.
II Corinthians 1:3–4 TLB

This is my comfort in my affliction,
for Your word has given me life.
Psalm 119:50 NKJV

Lord, I know I need to come before You
with clean hands and a pure heart. I confess
that right now I don't have either one.
Please cleanse me from my selfish motives
and my reckless tongue that seem to blindside me
and ruin my best intentions. Please replace
the weakness of my instincts with Your heart. AMEN

Who shall ascend the hill of the LORD? And who shall
stand in his holy place? He who has clean hands
and a pure heart, who does not lift up his soul
to what is false and does not swear deceitfully.
Psalm 24:3–4 ESV

Come close to God, and God will come close to you.
Wash your hands, you sinners; purify your hearts,
for your loyalty is divided between God and the world.
James 4:8 NLT

Because we have these promises, dear friends,
let us cleanse ourselves from everything that can defile
our body or spirit. And let us work toward
complete holiness because we fear God.
II Corinthians 7:1 NLT

Lord, seeing Your heart in Your Word is healing mine. Seeing Your strength is giving me confidence in You. Seeing Your faithfulness is giving me hope. Like Job, it seems like I had only heard about You before, but now I am seeing You with spiritual eyes. AMEN

I had heard of You [only] by the hearing of the ear,
But now my [spiritual] eye sees You.
Job 42:5 AMP

The Lord is near to the heartbroken and He saves those who are crushed in spirit (contrite in heart, truly sorry for their sin).
Psalm 34:18 AMP

Therefore know [without any doubt] and understand that the Lord your God, He is God, the faithful God, who is keeping His covenant and His [steadfast] lovingkindness to a thousand generations with those who love Him and keep His commandments.
Deuteronomy 7:9 AMP

Lord, as I count my blessings, I need to count every difficulty and loss that You have protected me from. I don't know what storm, illness, or accident I might have encountered without Your watchful care. I thank You for Your goodness toward me and the blessings of Your protections. AMEN

My help comes from the LORD, who made heaven
and earth. He will not allow your foot to slip;
He who keeps you will not slumber.
Psalm 121:2–3 NASB

You are my hiding place; You, LORD, protect me
from trouble; You surround me with songs
and shouts of deliverance.
Psalm 32:7 AMP

O give thanks to the LORD, for He is good;
For His lovingkindness endures forever.
I Chronicles 16:34 AMP

Lord, I am not doing very well today, and I feel helpless to encourage myself. My faith today is nothing that would make You proud. All I know to do is to confess what is true about You.

I may be weak, but You are strong. I am not hopeless because you sit at the right hand of the Father interceding for me. And I am not worthless because the Son of the Living God gave His life for me. AMEN

Therefore He is able, once and forever, to save those who come to God through Him. He lives forever to intercede with God on their behalf.
Hebrews 7:25 NLT

For God so loved the world that He gave His only begotten Son, that whoever believes in Him should not perish but have everlasting life.
John 3:16 NKJV

Lord, I wouldn't want to show my face to a friend without my make-up, but here I am face-to-face with You. What a comfort it is not to have to keep up any pretense, knowing that You see me just as I am. You know my weaknesses, my hopes, and my scars from life. And You know where I have blown it. Even beyond that, You know what my heart needs and how to help me. And You still love me. AMEN

As water reflects the face, so one's life reflects the heart.
Proverbs 27:19 NIV

For we are God's handiwork, created in Christ Jesus to do good works, which God prepared in advance for us to do.
Ephesians 2:10 NIV

And when you are praying, do not use meaningless repetition as the Gentiles do, for they suppose that they will be heard for their many words. So do not be like them; for your Father knows what you need before you ask Him.
Matthew 6:7–8 NASB

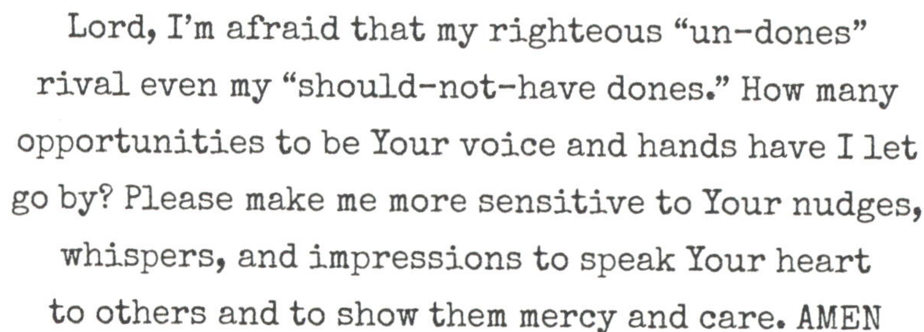

Lord, I'm afraid that my righteous "un-dones" rival even my "should-not-have dones." How many opportunities to be Your voice and hands have I let go by? Please make me more sensitive to Your nudges, whispers, and impressions to speak Your heart to others and to show them mercy and care. AMEN

But prove yourselves doers of the word,
and not merely hearers who delude themselves.
James 1:22 NASB

And do not neglect doing good and sharing,
for with such sacrifices God is pleased.
Hebrews 13:16 NASB

Don't just think about your own affairs, but be interested
in others, too, and in what they are doing.
Philippians 2:4 TLB

Lord, there is resentment in my heart from an offense and it is blocking the flow of Your grace and mercy through me. I am willing to let go of it—please take it from me! Help me keep this wound to my heart clean by not repeating what happened over and over in my mind. It would be easy for this wound to become infected with bitterness and anger. Then it would hurt me—and others—even more. I am choosing to cover it with forgiveness—help me keep that bandage on it as long as it takes to heal. AMEN

Look after each other so that not one of you will fail to find God's best blessings. Watch out that no bitterness takes root among you, for as it springs up it causes deep trouble, hurting many in their spiritual lives.
Hebrews 12:15 TLB

Hatred stirs old quarrels, but love overlooks insults.
Proverbs 10:12 TLB

A wise man restrains his anger and overlooks insults. This is to his credit.
Proverbs 19:11 TLB

Lord, when I finally see You in heaven someday, with a backward glance toward my earthly life, I will wonder, "What was all that stuff and busyness about?" And I will know that life on earth should have been about what heaven is about—all about You.

Constantly reset my compass to live in line with the rest of the universe so I will never have the regret of not realizing what life is about. I want You to be Lord over every day of my life—just as You are Lord over all of the universe. AMEN

He made the world and everything in it, and since He is Lord of heaven and earth, He doesn't live in man-made temples; and human hands can't minister to His needs—for He has no needs! He himself gives life and breath to everything, and satisfies every need there is.

Acts 17:24–25 TLB

Teach us to number our days and recognize how few they are; help us to spend them as we should.

Psalm 90:12 TLB

Lord, finally I realize that for some hopes there needs to be a death—a death for ideas and schemes that were never based on Your purposes and have wasted so much of my energy and time. I am willing to let all plans like that pass away so that I can experience Your plans for me with full joy and expectation, instead of wasting my days on unrealistic ambitions. I release every plan of mine that was never Your idea! AMEN

Commit your works to the Lord,
and your thoughts will be established.
Proverbs 16:3 NKJV

A man's heart plans his way,
but the Lord directs his steps.
Proverbs 16:9 NKJV

Lord, it is so, so easy to criticize others around me and assign blame to them. Please replace that pride in my heart with a desire to believe the best of others and to refuse to be an accuser. AMEN

And why do you look at the speck in your brother's eye, but do not consider the plank in your own eye? Or how can you say to your brother, "Let me remove the speck from your eye"; and look, a plank is in your own eye? Hypocrite! First remove the plank from your own eye, and then you will see clearly to remove the speck from your brother's eye.

Matthew 7:3–5 NKJV

So get rid of all evil behavior. Be done with all deceit, hypocrisy, jealousy, and all unkind speech.

I Peter 2:1 NLT

Yes, each of us will give a personal account to God. So let's stop condemning each other. Decide instead to live in such a way that you will not cause another believer to stumble and fall.

Romans 14:12–13 NLT

Lord, financial security is always a concern to me. The economy can fall and rise—only to fall again. It is unpredictable. But if all my money were to disappear today—and it might—I am trusting You. I can't imagine what that would be or how it would work, but it is You that has always been our provider, taking care of us even while we sleep.

AMEN

And my God will supply all your needs
according to His riches in glory in Christ Jesus.
Philippians 4:19 NASB

Stay away from the love of money;
be satisfied with what you have. For God has said,
"I will never, *never* fail you nor forsake you."
Hebrews 13:5 TLB

It is vain for you to rise early to retire late,
to eat the bread of anxious labors—For He gives
[blessings] to His beloved *even in his* sleep.
Psalm 127:2 AMP

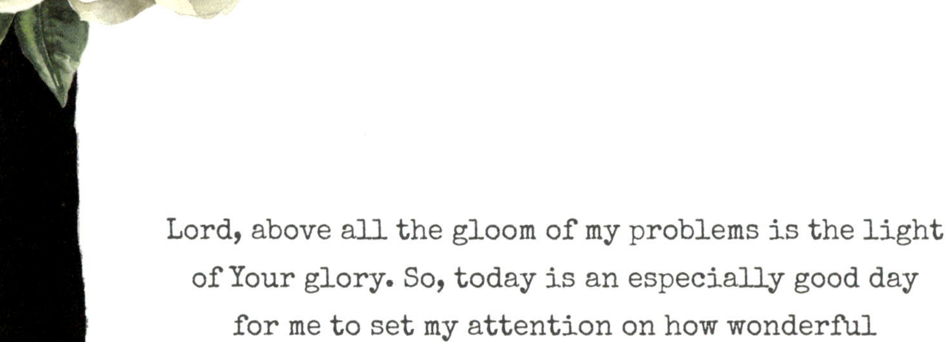

Lord, above all the gloom of my problems is the light of Your glory. So, today is an especially good day for me to set my attention on how wonderful You are and just worship You.

I praise You and I honor You for Your lovingkindness, mercy, wisdom and strength. For the brilliance of Your righteousness and holiness that reigns over all my circumstances. AMEN

On God my salvation and my glory *rest*;
The rock of my strength, my refuge is in God.
Psalm 62:7 NASB

Not to us, O LORD, not to us, but to Your name give glory
because of Your lovingkindness, because of Your truth.
Psalm 115:1 NASB

Lord, my world is so fluid. People are constantly trying to adapt to change and change themselves. I would be so hopeless and confused if You were changeable, but You are my rock. Whatever You say that You are—You always have been and always will be. Your name is I AM. AMEN

Jesus Christ is the same yesterday
and today and forever.
Hebrews 13:8 NASB

For I am the Lord—I do not change.
That is why you are not already utterly destroyed,
for My mercy endures forever.
Malachi 3:6 TLB

The grass withers, the flowers fade,
but the word of our God shall stand forever.
Isaiah 40:8 TLB

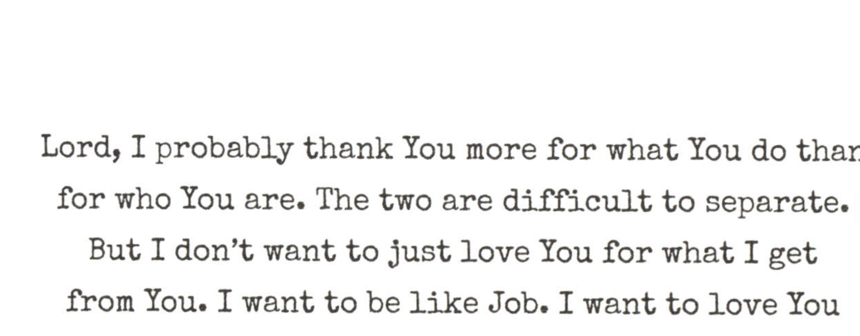

Lord, I probably thank You more for what You do than for who You are. The two are difficult to separate. But I don't want to just love You for what I get from You. I want to be like Job. I want to love You for Yourself—no matter what happens to me. AMEN

We love Him because He first loved us.
I John 4:19 NKJV

Jesus said to him, "You shall love the LORD your God with all your heart, with all your soul, and with all your mind."
Matthew 22:37 NKJV

You shall love the Lord your God with all your heart, with all your soul, and with all your mind.
Deuteronomy 6:5 NKJV

Lord, I am asking You to work in my heart layer by layer until I am not just *willing* for whatever You want, but until I really, deeply *want* what You want. This change is so difficult for me that I really need for You to do it by changing my heart. AMEN

I will give them a heart to know Me, for I am the LORD; and they will be My people, and I will be their God, for they will return to Me with their whole heart.
Jeremiah 24:7 NASB

You will seek Me and find Me when you search for Me with all your heart.
Jeremiah 29:13 NASB

And He said to him, "You shall love the LORD your God with all your heart, and with all your soul, and with all your mind."
Matthew 22:37 NASB

Lord, help me to teach my children how to "swim upstream" and not just float along with the crowd. Please give them courage they need to stand fast. Reveal Yourself to them in such a real way that they know in their hearts that Your love and Your plans for them are far above anything else that is being offered to them. Hour by hour, I ask You to keep me accountable to You so that no sin or attitude that would turn them away from You can find a place in my life. AMEN

In the same way, encourage the young men to live wisely. And you yourself must be an example to them by doing good works of every kind. Let everything you do reflect the integrity and seriousness of your teaching.
Titus 2:6–7 NLT

Train up a child in the way he should go [teaching him to seek God's wisdom and will for his abilities and talents], Even when he is old he will not depart from it.
Proverbs 22:6 AMP

We will not hide these truths from our children; we will tell the next generation about the glorious deeds of the LORD, about His power and His mighty wonders.
Psalm 78:4 NLT

Lord, the goal of my life is to be completely surrendered to You. That is the only way I know not to miss the blessings of everything You have planned for me. AMEN

For anyone who keeps his life for himself shall lose it; and anyone who loses his life for Me shall find it again.
Matthew 16:25 TLB

You can make many plans,
but the LORD's purpose will prevail.
Proverbs 19:21 NLT

Lord, I feel so inadequate to know how to truly worship You. You are wonderful in so many ways beyond my understanding and knowledge—even beyond words. My heart kneels in wonder. I crown You with words of praise and I honor You with my obedience. AMEN

I will exalt You, my God and King, and praise Your name forever and ever. I will praise You every day; yes, I will praise You forever Great is the LORD! He is most worthy of praise! No one can measure His greatness.
Psalm 145:1–3 NLT

Praise the LORD, my soul;
all my inmost being, praise His holy name.
Psalm 103:1 NIV

Lord, I don't want my hard days to just be
"survivable" or wasted time. Please make them
valuable days that I will always be grateful for—
days with memories of Your careful care to treasure.
Please use every challenge to deepen my trust
in You. Let others be encouraged that
You are watching and caring for me.

I have decided to not be passive—I will pray
and I will read Your Word and I will learn about Your
faithfulness in the lives of others while I am waiting
and enduring these days. AMEN

Therefore, do not throw away your confidence,
which has a great reward.
Hebrews 10:35 NASB

And we know [with great confidence] that God [who is
deeply concerned about us] causes all things to work
together [as a plan] for good for those who love God, to
those who are called according to His plan and purpose.
Romans 8:28 AMP

Consider it nothing but joy, my brothers and sisters,
whenever you fall into various trials. Be assured that
the testing of your faith [through experience] produces
endurance [leading to spiritual maturity, and inner peace].
And let endurance have its perfect result and do
a thorough work, so that you may be perfect and
completely developed [in your faith], lacking in nothing.
James 1:2–4 AMP

Lord, forgive me for tolerating the unimportant clutter in my life that clouds my focus. Forgive me for being satisfied with less than Your holiness in my life. Somehow the word "holy" seems so unreachable and so unattainable, but You have told me to be holy. You have made it possible for me to be holy because Your mercy has made it possible for me to be cleansed when I sin. So, I am purposely setting my heart on being set apart from everything that would keep me from You. AMEN

But now you must be holy in everything you do, just as God who chose you is holy. For the Scriptures say, "You must be holy because I am holy."
I Peter 1:15–16 NLT

Work at living in peace with everyone, and work at living a holy life, for those who are not holy will not see the Lord.
Hebrews 12:14 NLT

For God saved us and called us to live a holy life. He did this, not because we deserved it, but because that was His plan from before the beginning of time—to show us His grace through Christ Jesus.
II Timothy 1:9 NLT

Lord, I Need You: Prayers from a Humble Heart Devotional Journal

First Edition, May 2020
Published by:

21154 Highway 16 East
Siloam Springs, AR 72761
dayspring.com

Written by Sandy Lynam Clough
Artwork by Sandy Lynam Clough
Cover Design by Tyler Voss

Printed in Korea
Prime: J2029
ISBN: 978-1-64454-631-4